Playing Smart

The Professional Athletes' Handbook for Future Financial Stability

RYAN C. MACK

Playing Smart - *The Professional Athletes' Handbook for Future Financial Stability*

Copyright © 2014 by Ryan C. Mack

ISBN-13: 978-0-9859890-1-9

Library of Congress Control Number: 2014932455

TABLE OF CONTENTS

INTRODUCTION

ASK THE RIGHT QUESTIONS

Congratulations! You have just made the transition from an amateur athlete to a professional one. After the celebration has concluded you must come to terms with the new realities of your life. Here are two of those realities:

- Statistics show that the majority of you reading this will no longer be playing professionally five years from today and many will not have a plan for what you will do afterwards.

- While you must be happy with the salary you are earning now, too many of you won't have anything to show for it within five years after you are finished playing professionally.

The purpose of this manual is to ensure that you begin to prepare yourself for the financial issues that are coming your way and for your future. The following areas will be addressed in this manual:

- Wealth Management Principles
- Building a Team of Advisors

- Managing the 4 F's...Friends, Family, Fame, and Fortune
- Transitioning from Sports to Life
- Making an Impact
- Have Faith!

Permit me to share the following story:

There was a little boy who saw an elderly man sitting on a bench with a dog. The little boy walked up to the man and asked, "Hey old man...does your dog bite?"

The old man replied, "No. My dog don't bite."

"Are you sure?" asked the little boy.

"Yep...I'm sure," said the old man.

So the little boy went up to the dog and tried to pet it. Immediately the dog growled, jumped up, and bit the little boy on the hand.

"OUUUCH!!!!! Hey old man...I thought you said your dog don't bite!" the little boy yelled.

The old man said, "This ain't my dog."

*The moral to this story is one that we must apply to our financial lives ....**we must ask the right questions!***

As a first year professional athlete, you must know how to ask and get answers to the right questions. In this manual you will be given a series of questions and answers that you should know in order to be financially prepared for your future... not just those years when you are playing professional sports but a future beyond your athletic career. If you ask the right questions, get the right answers, and assemble the right plans, you will be able to accomplish this mission.

CHAPTER 1

WEALTH MANAGEMENT
PRINCIPLES

The legal, tax, and financial advising concerns of your new career will raise a variety of questions. Whether you are concerned with being more effective at preserving acquired wealth, planning your estate, or starting a business, it is imperative you have the answers to questions that will arise. <u>You and you alone are the primary person responsible for the management of your money.</u> Failure to appropriately manage your money will jeopardize your short and long-term goals, your long-term interests, your priorities and your overall welfare. I get it...I hear you saying that you are not an expert in this field. However, not being an expert in money management or finance or even worse, claiming to be too busy to give it your attention is not an excuse for not taking an active role and taking ownership of your financial plan. The following questions and answers will help you manage and control your long-term financial security and ensure the long-term preservation of your assets acquired from your career.

QUESTIONS

Do you think you are making too much money to budget?

"BALLIN'!" You hear the word in songs, day to day language, and clubs across America. It is very easy for a new professional athlete to get sucked into the fast life and/or celebrity world. A new house for mama, a new car, designer clothes, and wild personal spending can be addictive if left uncontrolled.

- Do you know how fast someone can spend a multimillion dollar salary that has already been chopped almost in half by taxes?

- What happens if you are sidelined by an injury but haven't saved your salary?

- Have you heard of a term called "money heaven"? This is a term that labels wherever you spend your money but never see it again…it goes into "money heaven".

- Did you know that your budget will help you to determine how fast you can meet your long-term financial goals? Do you know your financial goals?

- Which is worse? Going through the tedious task of writing out your budget with your advisors or being a part of the percentage of athletes who go broke after retirement because they never took the time to do it?

- If you shared your budget with your family as well as helped them to assemble a budget, wouldn't that make it easier to deal with their unsolicited requests for money?

Are you able to identify potential investment scams? Have you acquired a third-party review of your investment holdings?

I would love to tell you that all advisors are qualified, honest, and have a genuine concern for your well-being. However, if we learned anything from the dubious financial dealings of Bernie Madoff, some financial advisors are more concerned with the money they are making than the money you are protecting. It is YOUR job to protect yourself against this risk in order to protect your financial future.

- Have you hired a third-party financial firm or sought out a qualified party to review and analyze your investment statements?

- Can your investment advisor provide you with an independent third-party custodian report?

- Does your advisor plan on investing in trading firms that are not traded publicly?

Do you have a solid tax plan as a part of your overall wealth building strategy?

As much as we have seen celebrities and athletes get arrested and fined for tax evasion you certainly want to make sure you do all you can to ensure that Uncle Sam gets his money (although it goes without saying that you should absolutely use all the legal loopholes possible to minimize how much of your money Uncle Sam gets). You are now more than likely in a new tax bracket, will be traveling through many states with various state tax laws, and will have to deal with more tax laws than you had to deal with before your new career. <u>Turning your taxes</u>

over to a CPA and never paying attention to what you are paying is not an acceptable strategy!

- Have you thought about forming a corporation or partnership and having your income paid to it to receive tax savings?

- Does the CPA or tax specialist that you employ have a background of working with athletes?

- Can your tax advisor deal with international tax issues such as endorsement deals; or marketing income that comes from outside the US?

- Do you have a tax strategy that encompasses the taxes on your estate should you suffer an unlikely death?

Do you know if your investment strategy reflects the level of risk you are comfortable in taking and your personal value?

It bears repeating, handing over your investment matters to an advisor while you wash your hands of all responsibilities is the most unwise strategy you can pursue. You must have a working partnership with your advisor and take ownership of your investment activities. You must be the boss and the primary person responsible for your financial welfare!

- Did your advisor inform you of all your investment options? Did you listen?

- Have you gone to websites like www.fincalc.com and used their questionnaire: "What is My Risk Tolerance?" just to get an understanding of what the advisor should be doing?

- Are there social issues that matter to you that would impact your investment strategy? Do you not want to invest in tobacco, alcohol, or other companies that you deem to be immoral?

- Have you learned about the basics of investments? We know you are not an expert, but do you have the basic knowledge of investments so you can contribute to making an informed opinion about your investment portfolio?

Did you know that tax and investment issues can lead to legal issues? Do you have a good lawyer? (NO! Just because your agent is an attorney does not mean that he can handle all of your legal issues!)

Having a good lawyer who can proficiently represent you on many issues should never be underestimated.

- Do you have an attorney that can help you protect your assets, form a business, perform the background check of that potential "business partner" (that long lost cousin with the business scheme that needs your money), review operating agreements, or help deal with unexpected pregnancies?

Even though you are still young, do you have a good estate plan?

If you have never had or heard of an estate plan, you may not know the importance of one. However, your loved ones will certainly know the importance if, God forbid, you have an untimely death or disability. The younger you are and the fewer assets you have the more simple the estate plan will be, but it is still critical to have one. How will your assets be distributed if you pass away?

- Who will make the financial decisions for you if you are in a coma?

- Are your assets protected from creditors or from people who decide they want to sue you because they read about the size of your contract in the paper?

- Do you know how to draft a proper prenuptial agreement if you are getting married and concerned she could be marrying you for your money?

Have you considered insurance as a part of your financial plan?

The estate plan, budget, tax strategy, and insurance strategy are all important components of a financial plan. The ever growing world of insurance can be confusing and daunting. There is insurance tp cover the financial risk passing away pre maturely, cover your expenses if you are sick, cover the life of a partner in your business, cover the value of your home and other valuable assets, and much more. This strategy should not be approached one product at time, but as a comprehensive strategy.

- Does your family have enough money to cover your estate tax bill if you pass away?

- Is the insurance company that will provide the funding in your unlikely death or disability well capitalized and highly rated?

- Have you discussed with your estate planner and insurance agent the benefit of having your irrevocable trust own the insurance policy (as opposed to you) to remove the value of the life death benefit from your estate? Do you know what this means?

- Is the agent selling you a hefty insurance policy because he can make a hefty commission or do you really need that much insurance? Do you know how the agent is compensated?

How many steps have you taken to learn about the principles of financial planning?

I am not asking you to be an expert, but all of us must take some time to learn about these principles. <u>You must take ownership of your investment strategy</u>.

- How many classes have you taken to learn about financial planning?

- If you don't have time to take classes, how many books have you read about financial planning?

- If you don't have time to read books (which I find it hard to believe), how many articles online have you read on sites like Bloomberg.com, mint.com, learnvest.com, or others in order to educate yourself?

- I know you have been provided with resources in this area to make sure you are well informed, but often these resources are not used as much as they should be. Have you used the resources given to you? If there is anything that I can do to assist, please use me as a resource as well.

CHAPTER 2

BUILDING A TEAM OF ADVISORS

Now that you have made it, I want you to think of yourself as a business, a corporation of sorts. You are now like a business with tax issues, legal issues, business matters that need to be dealt with: exposure to risk and many opportunities comes to mind. Just like any successful business, you are able to delegate the responsibility of running some of your day to day operations to expert individuals who are most qualified to steer your "business" in the right direction. Yes, you may have an agent, but the agent is only qualified to deal with short-term solutions such as negotiating/securing contracts, getting large signing bonuses, and getting you those lucrative endorsement deals. However, as a business, you must think much larger and broader than the short-term transactions that can make you money. You must think about the long-term transactions that can grow your money and keep your money long after your career is over. After you leave your sports career and your endorsements run out, your agent will stop getting paid, but your advisory team has the potential to remain in your life forever.

QUESTIONS

Does the agent you are interviewing state that he is a one stop shop?

I would advise against allowing an agent to draw you into a relationship where he is the sole provider of the services you will require or where he will be the only person responsible for the selection of your financial team. Many times agents even charge a fee for the service of selecting those who will be helping you with other important matters. This represents a conflict of interest. Think about it…if you have one person who serves as your agent, manages investments, handles your tax planning, brings in business deals, and represents your legal matters, then who will ensure that this same person isn't selling services or products and promoting unnecessary services simply to make a commission.

- Do you have a separate legal advisor who can: give you guidance on how your various accounts should be titled, form corporations, provide asset protection, assist in a lawsuit, provide risk management, provide prenuptial planning, and whatever else that can come up?

- Did you know that just because an agent is also an attorney, he might not have the time to provide you the necessary legal services that you need beyond the scope of being an agent?

- Do you have a financial advisor who was not referred by your agent? A financial advisor who is referred by your agent might be inclined to give you advice that is only "approved" by the agent (since the agent referred him to you and he may want other referrals). Why would you work with someone who might be afraid of saying or doing something that may upset the agent?

- Do you have an independent tax advisor who can provide you great advice including the filing of your taxes as well as other issues that go far beyond tax season?

- Other than the necessary financial, tax, and legal advisor, I recommend you consider having a business consulting team member, a marketing team member, and/or a bookkeeper.

Have you properly reviewed the credentials/background of the advisors you are considering?

You are now in the realm of one of the most sought-after client bases in the country. You will never be able to go to a club, event, or out in public without the possibility of someone trying to solicit you as a client. The question is…how can you select the RIGHT advisor FOR YOU?

- That attorney you are considering…….have you researched whether or not he is a certified member of your state's bar association? Has their license ever been suspended, reinstated, revoked, or have they been disciplined for any reason?

- Have you looked up your financial advisor on www.finra.org AND on www.adviserinfo.sec.gov to see if they have been the subject of disciplinary action? Are they are a Certified Financial Planner or CFP?

- Have you checked on your CPA on www.aicpa. org to ensure they have not been the subject of any investigations? Are they a Certified Public Accountant or CPA?

- Did you get at least three reference checks from each advisor you are planning to hire? Have you followed up on all of references?

- Did you run a criminal background check on each potential advisor?

- Have you run across some credentials where there is no transparency or where you are unable to conduct a background check?

- What does this individual do outside their place of employment? Are they a family person, what school did they attend, and how active are they in their community?

- Is this person part of a large or a small firm?

- How much money did they make last year? Is their firm in financial trouble making them more likely to suggest products that make them money as opposed to what you really need? Have you seen a copy of their income statements (If they work for a publicly traded company you can find them online but if they don't, you should request them)?

- How did you feel when you interviewed the advisor? What was your gut telling you?

- Did you put together a team of three to five people with varying backgrounds who could help you interview the potential clients you will hire?

- Are you thinking of hiring a family member to be a crucial member of your advisory team (finance, legal, tax)? Think again! If your Uncle Leroy messes up your taxes how would your relationship fare by having to fire him? (Think of other roles they can play such as screen business opportunities, serve on your charity board, screen marketing deals, or something that can keep them busy but not be vital to your financial foundation.)

- Is the advisor so in awe of your celebrity nature that they can't or won't challenge you?

Who is the quarterback of your advisory team?

Your advisory team needs to be on one accord to ensure that you are not getting conflicting advice from various members of the team. Each decision made should be communicated to the others to ensure they are all on the same page. You must designate one member who is designated to look at the big picture which includes legal, marketing, planned giving, financial, and other important pieces of the puzzle. The "quarterback" then conveys the information to each of the advisors in a style that moves you towards reaching specific objectives and goals. Many times the quarterback is the legal firm you are working with; but that quarterback could also be your financial advisor especially if they are a CFP.

- YOU MUST KEEP IN MIND...regardless of whom you appoint as quarterback YOU are still the CEO of the firm and as such you must always be aware of what is happening with your team.

- Is there any member of the team who is inclined to operate in a vacuum and not collaborate with other members of the team? (You can EASILY find a replacement and you must make that clear from the onset.)

How is your advisor getting paid?

Everything should be transparent and above board as you are the one person issuing the checks with YOUR money.

- Is your investment advisor getting a fee of more than 1.5% of total assets under management? Is he asking for an upfront fee IN ADDITION to the assets under management fee? Example: If you give him $2 million to manage, he would be getting $30,000 (1.5% of $2,000,000) annually; PLUS, whatever he wants you to pay him as a retainer fee. In this hypothetical example you should ask him to waive the retainer fee altogether or you will find another advisor who is willing to do so.

- Is the investment advisor a "fee only" advisor, meaning that he does not get paid on commission products? If he is not, he could be more likely to put you into stocks to earn a commission for him as opposed to investments that might be more suitable for your needs.

- How much are you paying your CPA? The range of a CPA can be as low as $500 to $25,000 per year depending upon the complexity and frequency which you file your returns. You must know the amount of the total fees being charged by the CPA to determine if you are being overcharged.

- How much is the insurance agent getting paid? Is your financial advisor also licensed to sell insurance products? Do you know if you require the amount of insurance being suggested? Have you sought out a fee-based insurance advisor who will charge a fee and will not be paid a commission based upon the products that are sold to you?

- How much is your attorney charging you? Are they charging you between $200 and $1000 per hour which is typical or a flat fee for certain projects?

- Is your marketing consultant charging you more than 15% for any endorsement contract?

- Is your agent charging you more than three to four percent of your team salary?

CHAPTER 3

MANAGING THE 4 F'S ... FRIENDS, FAMILY, FAME, AND FORTUNE

It is an understatement that your life will change! The relationship with your friends (especially the new friends who will want to be in your circle) changes, and your family dynamics (including those you haven't seen in years) changes; and most of all the relationship with your parents changes. However, through careful management you can achieve the following three goals:

1. Stabilize and maintain those family relationships that you have nurtured all your life.

2. Insulate these relationships from the potentially negative impacts of money and fame.

3. Mitigate any potential risks that can jeopardize your financial security and long-term financial growth.

QUESTIONS

What are the boundaries you have set for your family?

There is nothing wrong with giving back to your family. I want you to give back to your family. However, you must learn early in the game to set boundaries for them. I understand the hard work your parents put into your life and I understand the expectations they have of you now that you have become a success. However, you and only you must now take on the task of fully understanding that a $1 million salary doesn't mean you will receive $1 million. Furthermore, a $1 million salary this year does not mean that you will be receiving a $1 million salary for the rest of your life. There is a relatively short time span that you will receive this income. It is time for you to make decisions that are based upon long-term planning, not short-term giving. Become adept at giving lines like, "Mom...I understand you want me to help you out more, but I have to ask you to save more of what I do give you. I am planning to take care of you for the rest of your life...not just the years I am in the league." How's that for some "game"?!

- Do you feel obligated to give back to your family who provided you love and support for many years? That is understandable, but can you give back to them in a way that is constructive and emphasizes personal responsibility?

- Have you held a family meeting with all your loved ones who you would like to help and laid out your financial plan? Perhaps you can let the "quarterback" be at this meeting so they can appear to be the "bad guy" when they find out that you will not be handing over blank checks every month? Does your family fully understand your plan, savings goals, and responsibilities so there are no misunderstandings?

- Does your family really understand your playing days are limited as well as your salary?

- Have you learned about and explained the impact of FICA, Medicare taxes, agent fees, state taxes, and federal taxes to your family?

- Is it possible to provide job opportunities as opposed to an allowance giving them an opportunity to earn their income? (Remember to steer clear of the primary pillars of your advisory team such as financial, legal, and tax advisor. Also, be sure that no matter what role you assign to a friend or family member, it is not a handout and they are qualified to do the job.)

- Have you thought about opening an account for your family, with your name on it as well, with a debit card and account statements mailed to you? This way you can monitor how the funds are being spent. Are you prepared to have that conversation with your family if you discover the funds are being spent on extravagant, unnecessary items as opposed to important items such as education, paying down debt, or basic living expenses?

- Can you remember that your family is not ENTITLED to your money and if you are a crutch for them today, you will forever be a crutch to them?

- Can you remember that you are the provider and if

you are no longer financially viable then you will no longer be able to provide for them or yourself?

- Have you told them they should never be able to call and ask for money during the season unless it is an emergency? If it is truly an emergency and it is during the season let your quarterback handle it - DON'T ALLOW YOUR FAMILY'S NON-EMERGENCY ISSUES TO DISTRACT YOU FROM YOUR TEAM RESPONSIBILITIES.

What is your plan for Cousin Ray Ray whom you haven't seen in 10 years?

People will come from all over (just like they would if you won the lottery) to get involved in your life again. Do you have a plan for these individuals?

- Can you be assertive enough to say no?

- Can you afford to give the money away? Lending money is the same as giving it away to friends and family because most often it never comes back.

- Have you notified your quarterback that they are to help you with large requests for loans? If you don't feel like being the bad guy, allow them to intercede and say "NO" to those people who are asking you to participate in risky financial transactions.

Can you remember who you are?

It can be easy to allow the fame and money to change the core of who you are, but it is necessary to remain grounded. Neon lights, limousines, autographs, women, money, and jewelry... all this can make it a daunting task to stay grounded.

- Can you remember to make less impulsive and self-centered decisions, and more rational and responsible decisions? Lean on your advisory team to assist you? The professional organization you are a part of undoubtedly also has a wealth of elder players who can mentor you in this process.

- Can you be comfortable with a modest home that you can afford AFTER your years of playing have ended?

- Do you enjoy being a celebrity more than you enjoy playing your sport? It costs a great deal more money to play the role of celebrity, but a good player - at your level - can be paid millions for your talents. Which one do you prefer?

When was the last time you called your mother?

It is one thing to set financial boundaries, but financial boundaries are by no means social boundaries. One must make an effort to remain in touch with family members and loved ones. This can go a long way to keeping you grounded as well as keeping those who matter the most to you close. Those you meet on the road will come and go, but your family is with you forever.

Keep family and business separate?

Your Uncle may be a great financial advisor, but can you fire him if he makes a bad decision? Perhaps you can put him on the pay role for a far lesser price to be a paid consultant who works with your other advisors on the team in case you can't return a call in a timely manner?

Have you used your funds to teach your family how to fish?

It is one thing to give money to a family member, but it is another to invest in their future in a responsible way within your budget. Start thinking long-term and see how you can use this opportunity and blessing to make a better way for your family that will last generations. I have attached an article about the "Economic Value of Family" in the appendix of this manual. Read it and start to put a plan of action in place to empower your family and show them what a leader you have become.

CHAPTER 4

TRANSITIONING FROM SPORTS TO LIFE

Most of you reading this will not be playing professional sports five years from today. However, for the sake of argument, let's say that you are an anomaly and that you are playing in your sport after the age of 35. At that point you will have lived about one third of your life...what's next? The preparation for "what's next" starts right now...in this first year playing in your sport. The earlier you start, the more seamless you will be able to make that transition into the next phase of your life. There are three critical factors that will shape your transition:

1. The business deals you choose to invest in.

2. The education you choose to pursue.

3. The network you choose to establish.

QUESTIONS

"I have a great business deal that should give a huge return...do you want in?" How will you respond to this question?

The money you are earning presents a unique opportunity to invest in a variety of ventures that can appeal to your passion in life as well as make additional money. Significant returns, great long-term value, a sense of self-worth, confidence, and a feeling of pride are all benefits of being involved in a successful venture that will follow you into retirement from playing professionally. However, starting a business is also the most risky investment one can pursue and it is imperative that you take the necessary time to review each opportunity and have a clear perspective.

- Do you consider yourself an expert in the proposed business; or do you at least have some knowledge of it? How much time have you taken to learn about the opportunity being presented to you?

  - I am not suggesting that you should be an expert, but you should NEVER invest your money if you don't have a clear understanding of the proposed opportunity.

- Have you run this idea past your advisory team to allow them to conduct a thorough analysis of the deal/investment?

  - You will need to use that superstar advisory team you have formed to give you an expert analysis. Keep in mind that there could be a conflict of interest to have only your financial planner give an overview of the investment opportunity. He may not want to withdraw funds from that same investment account paying him.

- Is there a time limit on this business deal or investment that requires a quick decision?

  - There is no such thing as a business deal that won't ever come again and requires you to act in haste. If you don't have the time to do proper due diligence, then you should pass on the deal/investment.

- Have you taken the time to set up your financial, legal, and tax plans yet?

  - Before you assume a high risk investment you must first determine how much risk you are able to take on. This is done by setting up your financial strategy. <u>Don't invest in any business venture or investment unless you have established your financial, estate, and tax plans.</u>

- Are you comfortable with not seeing a profit from your investment over a period of years? On the other hand, if you lose all of your money in this investment, will it jeopardize your long-term goals and lifestyle needs as outlined in your financial plan?

- Will you be a "silent" or an "active" investor?

- Have you relied upon the expertise of the person presenting the deal or have you hired your own business consultant? THIS IS A MUST (in addition to having your Advisory Team review it)!

- <u>If you are questioning the necessity of paying money for a consultant</u>...would you rather pay $2500 for a consultant or lose $250,000 on an outlandish business venture masked in a professional looking 30 page proposal.

- Does the business consultant you hire have the ability to review financial statements?

- What happens if the business goes into default...are you liable for any of the debt?

  ◆ Will you be held liable if the company issues a capital call from a bank?

- Have you thought about asking for additional consideration and ownership since your name and likeness will be used to attract more investors?

- What does your gut say about the person offering the investment and the deal itself?

- Will this deal have a negative or positive impact on your image?

- Has your business consultant done a thorough background check on the person offering the deal and all partners, members, and shareholders involved? (Resumes, references, checked social media pages, video clips, criminal history, pending lawsuits, litigation, credit report, etc.)

- Have you talked with your legal team to ensure the company is set up with the appropriate legal structure?

Have you pursued an education?

For those who have not earned a college degree I want you to understand that within the next ten years you will probably be retired from your professional athletic career and might need a degree to increase the odds of your employment. For those who have a degree, understand the road to advancing your education is perpetual. Playing professional sports should not negate the necessity to get additional education.

- Have you started to read about careers or business ventures you would like to pursue after your days of playing professionally are over?

- If you haven't received your degree, have you enrolled in college courses to pursue your education? Have you talked with career counselors at local colleges about various career opportunities?

Who's in your network of friends?

Oftentimes your friends define your aspirations and/or people perceive you as being like those you are with most often. I am not suggesting that you give up your friends from the neighborhood or your hometown. I am suggesting that you establish a network of friends who understand the expectations of your career and who will support you now and into the future (don't be surprised if there are not many of these). As they say in my neighborhood, "You may have to drop somebody!" In other words, not everyone will be able to take this journey with you.

- Within your network of friends, do you find many people who are educated, driven, and are independently working towards something on their own? Or do you have many "yes" men and women who want to hang around you simply because of your status?

♦ At this stage in your life you must be critical of the "new" people who come into your circle and assess whether or not they can help or hinder your progress. If you are the smartest person in your circle, you need to find a new circle!

CHAPTER 5

MAKING AN IMPACT

You have an enormous opportunity to make a difference by giving your time or money. However, it must be done in a way that doesn't jeopardize the security of your long-term financial security. Let me share with you a brief poem:

SELF

I would rather help you than help self.

But I cannot help you unless I can help self.

So that I can better help you I need to help self.

Self-empowerment and community empowerment can be synonymous as long as you are doing it because of personal responsibility and not greed. Greed prohibits an individual from thinking about others, and personal responsibility ensures that you will do what is necessary to position yourself to empower others. There is an opportunity for you to create a legacy of community empowerment as long as you carefully plan and prepare for it.

What are you passionate about?

Would you like to help kids in your community learn the value of reading, help raise funds to find a cure for cancer, work with people in prison and reduce recidivism, or help veterans returning home find jobs? All these things can make an impact to a cause that is larger than you.

- Other than your athletic talent, name five skills, talents, or hobbies that you possess. What are some hot topics that get you excited to discuss?

    ◆ These could all be tapping into your passion.

- Have you considered starting a foundation or a charity? Have you talked to your legal team to discuss the process?

    ◆ As a person of influence you have an opportunity to be a trendsetter or a change agent in your community.

- If you don't want to give money, have you considered giving time?

    ◆ Your presence can make a difference in the lives of those who view you as a role model. Embrace this new life...whether the cameras are on you or not.

- And by the way...did you maximize all the tax deductions on your giving?

CHAPTER 6

HAVE FAITH

With faith, nothing is impossible. Faith is how you got to where you are today; faith is how you will be able to sustain a successful life after you have retired from professional sports; and any goal you desire can come true through faith. Faith is not rainbows, unicorns, and other notions of false realities. Faith is effort, faith is diligence, faith is real, and faith is hard work! You can read hundreds of self-empowerment books but if you choose to believe that the principles are not for you, you will not be successful. You must believe that there is not only a greater quality of life for you, but also for your family and your community. One of your most important tasks is to contribute towards making a better world. The best way to do that is to make a better you.

FINAL QUESTIONS

Do you know what faith is?

There is a simple equation that defines faith: Faith = ½ Belief + ½ Action

- Do you want to be in debt five years after you have left your career as a professional athlete?

- Do you want to depend upon others for your financial security after your retirement because you have spent all your money and failed to plan/execute a financial strategy?

- Do you have faith that you can be a success not only as a professional athlete, but as a professional in another chosen field after you sports career is over?

You must believe that you will be successful after your years as a professional athlete are over and you must act on that belief. In essence you must have faith that your actions will result in a good future for you, your family and your community.

What we have been describing within this document are the questions necessary to take the actions to start you on the road towards fiscal responsibility. There are many who care about your future, I care and want to help, but most importantly you need to care. I look forward to seeing faith in action as you make the plans necessary to create your financial strategy!

CHAPTER 7

NEXT STEPS

From this day forward I urge you to always make the following goal a priority:

"My GOAL is to be financially comfortable now and to be financially secure after I have retired from playing professional sports".

With this goal in mind, here is what you must do starting RIGHT NOW:

1. **Write out your budget** – Can you live on an after-tax $50,000 - $75,000 per year budget or 10% of your total gross annual salary for at least the first two to three years of your playing career? You must create a written budget that includes all your estimated expenses (i.e. travel, crucial/necessary family expenses, rent or mortgage, car expenses, clothing, entertainment, financial support for other family, etc.). Keep in mind that living according to this budget will maximize the possibilities for a comfortable retirement. Yes, you will be living

modestly but trust me, you will thank me for it later.

a. **Stick to your budget** and include all financial help to friends and family members WITHIN the 10% of your salary that you are spending for those first two to three years. So if $750,000 is your yearly salary, then $75,000 is your yearly allocation for all expenses, and the rest you should put towards savings...financial support to friends and family support should come from the 10% yearly allocated expenses and NOT from the money you are saving for your future. REMEMBER YOUR GOAL – <u>financial security after retirement.</u>

2. **Write out your financial goals** – It is often said, "Where there is no vision the people perish." Write out your financial goals which should include major purchases such as a house and/or a car and most importantly a nest-egg for your retirement. I know many of you want to have those fancy big ticket items (i.e. boats, expensive watches, etc.) and I am not saying that you should not buy them. I just want to make sure you purchase them within your means while not putting your more important long-term financial goal at risk.

3. **Assemble a Support Team** – Take some time to assemble two to four individuals whom you trust and who will be available to support and counsel you. This Support Team consists of professional and experienced people in your network (i.e. family, trusted friends, colleagues) that have the experience

to help you interview and select your Core Team of Advisors. Remember, there are many veterans in your organization who are willing to assist you with this process...use their wisdom and guidance and, just as important, learn from their mistakes. Your Support Team will serve as a sounding board to help you navigate through the challenges and pitfalls of being a professional player.

4. **Select your Core Team of Advisors** – The "core four" consists of your <u>agent, financial advisor, accountant, and attorney</u>. Use this handbook to help you determine which questions you should be asking. If you haven't found a complete team of advisors that you can trust, don't worry too much about it. I would rather you take your time to get it right, than to rush and make a decision to select an advisor that is not a good fit for you. Just get a relationship with a personal banker who can, FOR FREE, make sure you are stacking your savings into your savings account. (Remember you are trying to live on 10% of your salary for the first two years...the rest you should be stacking even if it is in a simple savings account). Remember these two points that bear repeating multiple times.

   a. *YOU ARE THE BOSS* OF YOUR ADVISORY TEAM – Yes, they are the experts and know more than you about their craft. However, <u>THEY WORK FOR YOU</u>! If you don't understand something make them repeat it. If you feel they are talking too fast or above your head...make them slow down or come down to your level. If they are unwilling they you should be unwilling to remain a paying client and fire him/her!

b. *KEEP INVOLVED* – It is NOT ACCEPTABLE that you do not know what your financial advisor is doing with YOUR MONEY. I am not asking that you be an expert, but I am asking you to stay involved...ask questions and meet/ talk with them on a regular basis. Remember, even Oprah Winfrey - who is a billionaire - still signs each one of her checks.

5. **Check your credit** – Go to www.annualcreditreport. com and get copies of your credit reports and have someone assist you as you go over them. Before you even ask...the answer is NO...you DO NOT have to pay someone to do this. I am willing to assist you, more than likely there are many resources in the organization or league you play for who would be willing to assist you, or you can use FREE services such as www.crown.org to get assistance in reviewing your credit report. You want to check for errors, check for any debts that you didn't know about, and make sure that you get into the habit of keeping it clean. You get one free credit report each year from Experian, Equifax, and Transunion so be sure to use this free service. I am sure there will be many who tell you that you need to pay for this service...not true.

6. **Talk to your family** –It is imperative that you sit down with your family and share your vision. Include your Support Team in this meeting so everyone is on the same page and everyone is knowledgeable

of your goals. It isn't necessary to give them details of your budget but let them know that you will be spending only a small portion of your monthly income, especially for the first two years. Let them know the most important goal for you is to have financial security after you retire. Remember these important points when dealing with family and ask for help from your Support Team if necessary:

a. It is very easy to enable someone to become financially dependent on you. In fact it sometimes makes us feel good that we can help. In reality, however, we are not doing that person a favor by encouraging financial dependency. If you want to do something, make sure it is within your monthly budget.

b. Don't be cold, but learn how to say no; saying no to a family member does not mean that you do not love them.

c. Believe it or not some people (especially family members) can become too burdensome with their requests for money and subsequent anger with your responses of "No". You should keep in mind that there are some people like this and they must simply be ignored. Just because someone is in your heart does not mean they should also be in your life...some people you need to learn to love from a safe distance. Years later when you are living a life of true financial security with more of a means to assist them, without hindering your own future financial goals, they will understand.

7. **Pay off all your credit card debt.** Most credit card debt is used for items that depreciate in value and leave you with tons of debt. Use your new found prosperity to eliminate debt you have racked up in the past. If you must help family members, pay off a family member's debt ONLY if the money you spend is within your monthly budget. This is much better and more practical than giving cash that may or may not be spent responsibly. If a family member continues to rack up additional debt, it is a clear indication that they are not living within their means and has problems that can't be fixed simply by you throwing money at it.

8. **Max out your organization's retirement program contributions** – If your organization or league has one, take advantage of it.

9. **Establish a time when you will meet with members of your Advisory Team** – individually or as a group. This meeting and the time designated for the meeting(s) will be SACRED. Under no conditions should you or they cancel this meeting. It is your time to be informed about YOUR BUSINESS (i.e. what's happening with your investments, etc.).

Other points to keep in mind:

- **DO NOT give ANYONE full power of attorney.** Talk to your attorney about this.

- **Be cautious of all insurance products you purchase.** NEVER sign the dotted line of any insurance product without having your Support Team read the policy, discuss it with you and with the agent. Remember, you are planning to live, not to die. I have seen too many of you over invest in some pricey insurance products, fattening the pockets of the agent who gets a commission, and tying up too much money that should be going towards your long-term financial plans/goals. Talk to your financial advisor and your Support Team about how much insurance (and what kind of insurance) you need.

- **Plan an annual performance review and strategy session with your team of advisors**. Once per year you should assemble your entire team of advisors with your Support Team to sit down and evaluate how effective they have been in achieving your financial objectives. In addition, as a unit they must discuss your future financial plans and objectives in a manner you can understand. Keep in mind your long-term goal is to have financial security after retirement – everyone should be working towards this goal.

- **Write out your will**, living will, health care proxy, and a durable springing financial power of attorney (much different from a regular power of attorney as it only applies in those times when you are deemed by a court to be unable to make financial decisions for yourself).

- **Be skeptical of risky investments**. Put record labels, nightclubs, restaurants, and other high risk investments on your "forbidden list" until you have had at least two to three years in the league. At that time you should only invest monies into investments that you CAN AFFORD TO LOSE without compromising your long time financial plan (remember your goal of financial security after retirement). **Walk away from all propositions that sound too good to be true**

- **Keep getting educated in finance.** Turn off "Love and Hip Hop" and turn on CNBC from time to time. Each morning when you wake up, read the front page of finance.yahoo.com or www.bloomberg.com for five minutes to get exposed to the language of financial literacy.

- **Build your circle of smart people** - People who understand your goals and support you in achieving them!

- **Remember this line** – <u>Just because you have the money, doesn't mean you have to spend the money!</u> One of the major causes of "going broke" is the inability to gauge cash outflow effectively. $20,000 here...$10,000 there...$5000 over there... these expenditures individually may not seem like much but they certainly add up over time. Stop the flooding before it starts and *stick to your budget*! <u>Don't be the athlete who two years after retirement is wondering, "Where did all my money go?!"</u>

- **Repeat all steps above continuously!**

Lastly you must understand the importance of "net worth". Net worth is all of your assets (what you own) MINUS your liabilities (what you owe). Whether on a downloaded worksheet that you fill out or with the help of your advisor, calculate your net worth. Your net worth will determine how much of your salary you can spend in order to accumulate enough for a secure financial future – your main goal. <u>Remember this; if your net worth isn't at least 20 times your annual expenses then you have no real financial security.</u> Therefore, if you want to spend $200,000 per year, your net worth should be at least $4,000,000 (assets = house, car, savings, investments, etc. MINUS all debt).

Do any of those suggestions sound like rocket science? No! None of this is hard, but we must not underestimate the importance of getting them accomplished. You have many resources at your fingertips…too many to allow crucial mistakes to pile up. I want you to have a true "balling" lifestyle, but I don't want you to have it if it can only exist supported by debt. You have seen what's happened to others who amassed excessive debt to support a lifestyle of lavish spending well beyond their means…learn from their mistakes. It might take a second, but if you follow the above steps and continue to learn and educate yourself, you might not become as good at finances as you are with your sport…but the odds of you building a long lasting financial legacy have significantly increased. I wish you the best of luck!

APPENDIX A

FINDING ECONOMIC VALUE IN FAMILY

The strongest role of any economic recovery comes from within the households across the country. It is up to each of us to determine how to use our skills, maximize our talents, and fully recognize and implement the resources in our communities to move forward economically. One of the most precious and under-utilized resources is the family.

That's right…the family. Those people who together cry at funerals, rejoice at weddings, celebrate birthdays, stuff themselves at holidays, and reminisce at reunions. The family for many is a place to find solace from the tough economic challenges of society. After going through stressful times there is nothing better for me than to take a trip back to my hometown of Detroit to where all is familiar. However, if we only look at the family for shelter we are missing the mark. This familiarity has with it enormous economic potential. In a world where love, trust, dedication towards one another, and sensitivity can be void…these traits are more likely to be found within your own family. However, we must maximize its potential and take advantage of the "family empowerment program".

Step One – The Family Callout

Contact your family and let them know you would like to select a date at least six months in advance to organize a Family Empowerment Meeting. Your family consists of all of your immediate family, extended family, and close friends that you consider family.

Step Two – Select a Date

Select dates for the meeting that would allow many of your family to attend. Try to accommodate as many family members as possible, but understand that it will be next to impossible to accommodate all as travel can be hard to coordinate. Perhaps you can organize the meeting around a date where the family is already getting together such as a holiday or a reunion? What I have done in organizing other family meetings is try to get as many as possible to commit to a date, then utilize technology such as Skype or a free conference call service. By using technology those members who cannot participate in person can still take part in the conversation. Pull together a committee of no more than five people that will assist in the selection of this date and planning an agenda so the topics of discussion will be limited…we all know what can happen when we have "too many cooks in the kitchen".

Step Three – Select an Objective/Unbiased Moderator

For this meeting it is important to choose someone outside the family that you trust to moderate the discussion. This person's task is only to make sure the discussion goes smoothly. They should be outside the family so they can be objective and not have a biased view. I could never be the moderator for my family because to many I am still seen as "Little Ryan" and an opinion or instruction given from me will not be viewed the same as an unbiased third-party even if that opinion/instruction is exactly the same. To reiterate, the moderator's job is NOT to show favoritism, but to make sure the conversation runs smoothly.

Step Four – Give the Meeting a Professional Structure

The structure of the meeting should the same as a business meeting, not a casual family gathering. Here are a few tips:

- There should be someone taking minutes of the meeting.

- The moderator must give the rules of engagement at the beginning of the meeting...the primary rule being that nobody speaks unless they are recognized to speak by the moderator.

- Think about a board meeting you may have attended and devise rules for your family. Email/mail these rules and a meeting agenda to all members of the family at least a week prior to the meeting to ensure that everyone is on the same page.

Your family should know that this meeting is about BUSINESS and not PLEASURE!

Step Five – Ask the Right Questions

The questions that are asked and follow up responses are the most important part of the meeting. Here are some great questions that should be asked by the moderator for the family meeting and ones that I have asked in the past:

- *Who needs a job?*
  - ◆ As hands rise have the secretary record the names of those looking for employment.
  - ◆ Ask each person who raised his/her hand to state which type of job they desire.
  - ◆ As each person gives the type of career they are pursuing have the moderator ask the rest of the family if they are able to provide assistance in finding a position in their desired field.
    - Eg: Cousin John is looking for a job in custodial services...is there anyone in the family who can assist Cousin John in finding this type of position?

Many people are able to find employment within their own families. A resume submitted to Monster.com is great but nothing works better than having someone on the inside pushing hard to get you that position.

- *Who is in danger of foreclosing their home?*
  - ◆ If hands rise have each one get up and tell their reasons for going into foreclosure.
  - ◆ If the reason is neglect then family assistance may not be the desired option. However, if the reason is for other legitimate reasons (illness, loss of employment, etc.) here are a few solutions the pooled resources of the family can provide:
    - A collection of funds and A PLAN put together to ensure the mortgage is paid.

- If there are others in the family that rent in the area perhaps they can move into the home and pay rent to the homeowner.

Passing legacy from generation to generation is crucial and maintaining home ownership is one of the best ways to do it.

- *Are there any youth under the age of 18 who plan on going to college?*
  - ◆ Using resources like a 529 plan can be a great means of building tax free/deferred college savings.

Scholarships are great but they can't always be relied upon. Through the pooled resources of the family we can start to create our own scholarships for our youth.

- *Do we have any business owners in the family that need support or people who would like to start a business?*

Many times we don't know the businesses that exist within our own families. These should be the first businesses that you support. You never know...there could be a family business waiting to be formed full of employment opportunities for everybody if the business is nourished well.

If you can think of any other questions that are pressing be sure to prepare all of them in full and distribute them along with the rules and meeting agenda.

> **NOTE**
>
> Have each member prepare a list of resources in their community they are aware of that provide great services in job training, employment, career development, drug rehabilitation, services for the formerly incarcerated, or any other important services various members of your family could find useful. Have them bring this list to the meeting and give it to the secretary. Compile this list of important resources on your own family site using a Facebook.com Group, a Linkedin.com Group, or a personally designed free website for your family using Wix.com. Begin to compile this "family resource list" at a central location for all to use.

Step Six – Select a Community Nonprofit to Adopt

The economic recession of the mid 2000's took a toll on the smaller nonprofits in our communities all across this nation. These smaller nonprofits are doing great work in educating our children, reforming those who were formerly incarcerated, feeding the homeless, providing aide to veterans, and much more. At the meeting, the family should vote on a cause they would like to champion, choose a local nonprofit that works to fulfill that need, and as a family decide upon the type of family support will be given that nonprofit. This support can come in the following ways:

- Pooling of funds to make donations
- Volunteering time to support an initiative
- A mixture of both

Step Seven – Follow Up

This meeting should occur at least once per year with regular updates of the positive stories that have come out of these meetings. If someone finds a job, send an email to the group, call others to provide that positive testimony, or send out postcards reminding people of the value in continuing to look out for one another. I have seen employment found, homes saved, and family wealth saved from family empowerment meetings I have hosted/moderated in my community. This program works! There is nothing that is greater to build a family bond than working together for the benefit of the community.

I know many reading this are thinking, "This sounds really great on paper but I will never be able to get my family to do all of this." I beg you to check your negativity at the door. Sure, it might not be normal for your family to do this, but aren't you tired of having problems such as high unemployment as the norm within the limits of your family? Our families have hurt far too long and the best answer will not come from the government but from right under our noses. None of us is as strong as all of us, and if we work together there is nothing we can't do to move our families, communities, and country forward…one family at a time!

APPENDIX B

GIVING TO YOUR FRIENDS/ FAMILY RESPONSIBLY

Too many times in family communities across the country those who have become comparatively financially successful are unknowingly volunteered to become the "universal provider" within their family circle. I should stress the word "comparatively" because many times those who are MORE successful within a family are also having their own financial problems, but because they do not exhibit the same signs of struggle as other family members often they are viewed as "well off". The universal provider is constantly hit with requests for short-term loans that should never be called loans because somehow they are never repaid. These pleas for assistance from family members in need, affectionately known as Ray-Ray sound something like this:

> "I am a little short on rent this month…can I borrow $500 until I get my tax return?" (Which never comes.)

> "I was laid off from work again…can I borrow $2000 until I can get back on my feet again?"

"I was evicted from my apartment…can I stay in your place rent free until I can find another place to live?"

I am NOT saying that people should not help others; however, it is time for us to speak candidly about how we are helping our close friends and family members. If you constantly find yourself in the role of the "universal provider" issuing "loans" that are never paid back then my argument is you are not helping anybody at all. You are enabling their dependence upon you as opposed to helping them develop their own ability to sustain their economic well-being. Furthermore, many universal providers are suffering from their own economic hardships and this irresponsible giving can precipitate their economic demise as they squander the precious few dollars they had stored for living expenses, bills, or even retirement and other important long-term goals. So for the universal providers out there, here are three tips to maximize the resources in your family:

1. **Use a creative promissory note** – Make sure that every time Ray-Ray asks you for a loan there is a written agreement before funds exchange hands. This agreement is to outline the terms of the loan, such as how the loan will be paid back, the timeframe of the loan, and conditions if the loan is defaulted. The agreement is to be signed by both parties. Do not be afraid to enforce this agreement in a court of law. I understand this can feel cold, but it is even colder if Ray-Ray does not pay back a debt and you find yourself in a financial bind. You don't have to request to be paid back in monetary terms but perhaps an exchange of man hours applied to household chores, errands for your business, or even

community service hours donated to your favorite local nonprofit.

You can also request to be paid back with documented proof of Ray-Ray's efforts to improve his condition. Proof of enrollment in the local community college, evidence of a completed website for his new business, a written letter from a GED program to complete a high school degree, copies of completed job applications... all of these are evidence of tangible tasks that this individual is actually doing work to improve their economic condition. If they are not able to provide this proof then it is time to take them to see Judge Mathis! The bottom line is there must be a measure of accountability. Without accountability Ray-Ray will continue to tap your financial well until it runs dry leaving you both penniless and dependent upon the next family member to waste their crucial financial resources.

2. **Have a family empowerment meeting** – One of the most powerful financial support systems within our communities, if we are efficient and not irresponsible in how we utilize the resources, is the family. I think we take for granted how powerful the family is. Families are great at meeting for Easter, Christmas, weddings, funerals, reunions and other normal gatherings; however, what if the family could meet specifically to have economic empowerment discussions?

I have hosted many family meetings where we are able to seek and find the necessary empowerment resources within the family. Pull ALL the members of the family together including immediate, extended, and close friends who are just like family. Have an independent person who knows a bit about finance host the discussion (preferably someone you can trust to not think of this as an opportunity to make a sale) and answer direct questions such as the following:

- How many people are unemployed and within what fields do you have an expertise or skills? Have someone take notes of those who respond then follow up with the question, "Do we have anyone in those particular fields that can assist with a connection or resource to assist?"

- Do we have any children who are going to college and can we all agree to establish a college savings fund in a 529 account in which we pool funds for those youth going to school?

- Is there anybody who is in jeopardy of foreclosure or being evicted? Can we set up a roommate situation to save the home or pool funds for a mortgage in return for in-kind services rendered?

- Do we have any current or future entrepreneurs in the family who need support and can you outline exactly the type of support you will need from the family? Is there a possibility to turn any of these business ideas into family run businesses by which we all can profit?

3. **SAY NO!** – If you don't have the money, guilt is not a good enough reason to try to come up with

the money. Learning how to say no is one of the easiest yet most difficult things we need to do in our community.

If you really want to help somebody, putting them in a position where they can help themselves is the most effective way of providing assistance. Giving them money is just putting gum in the hole of the dam which may seem to stop the leak temporarily, but only leads to a larger crack and ensuing flood when the dam breaks which hurts everybody. Tough love must be tough, but it must be balanced by love so don't ever turn down a chance to help those you love. Find a way to help that will lead to true empowerment and all of your family will be stronger for it in the end!

APPENDIX C

SELECTING THE RIGHT ADVISOR AND BUILDING YOUR FINANCIAL TEAM

Excerpt Taken from "*Living in the Village*" Written By Ryan Mack

During the holiday season of 2007, the year of the worst recession since the Great Depression, I remember watching the news about "Black Friday," the day after Thanksgiving. A person was trampled to death by shoppers who were just too excited to get into the store to find the biggest deal. What have we come to in this country when we kill someone because of a sale? What if we were just as excited about purchasing things that will actually improve upon our lives as opposed to add no value, decrease our savings, and increase our debt? What if we were that excited about getting a financial advisor that we can trust who will help us to figure out a path to financial freedom, early retirement, fully funded college savings, a new home, anew business, and eliminating all of our debt?

Those who are rich understand the importance of making

investments in those things that add value. This is why 5% of the country owns 95% of the wealth --they do the things necessary to retain wealth and not squander it. A good financial advisor can help you do this too. The best way for you to prepare for retirement, how to properly plan for your estate, how to discern the right amount of insurance to protect your family, planning to start a business, and assisting you to reach those important financial goals in your life are all things that should be covered by a good advisor. If you are not familiar with how to navigate through many of the tough financial obstacles that plague you, or if you are financially savvy but like most of us don't have the time to put together and monitor a comprehensive financial plan it is a wise move to ask for assistance. The hardest part of the process is selecting the best advisor for your needs. Below are a few questions to ask the financial advisor to make sure they are a good match for you:

Do you have a CFP?

To be a Certified Financial Planner is the exam that is the equivalent to the CPA for accountants but for Financial Planners. They are required to complete a series of requirements that include education, experience, ethics, and an exam. This exam proves that they actually know the curriculum of financial planning. Suze Orman, even though I have never actually met her, is a CFP. There are great advisors who do not have a CFP who are qualified, but your job is to lessen the odds of choosing an advisor who is not qualified...to select one who has one increases the odds that they are.

Can I see a copy of your ADV?

Every Registered Investment Advisor must register with the

state security agency or the SEC. This will tell you how the advisor is compensated, incentives that they are entitled to, educational and business background, and investment strategy. If the person cannot produce their ADV, then walk away.

If the firm gets paid by selecting investments on commission, which you can find out on the ADV, then I would suggest that you not use them and find a "fee-only" advisor. This advisor has no conflict of interest when suggesting which securities you should invest in, or if you should be investing at all. I remember when I was talking with an advisor and I asked him why they didn't sell any no-load mutual funds for their clients and his response was simply, "How are we supposed to get paid?" I have met many individuals who were coerced to purchase investments even though they had over $10,000 in credit card debt paying 18% interest. Does it make sense to put money in the stock market to HOPEFULLY earn an 18% return when you have a certain 18% payment in credit card debt? Absolutely not! You want an advisor who can see that and not be motivated to have you purchase stocks just so they can earn a commission.

Can I obtain at least three referrals from clients that you have worked with?

This is important because nobody will have a greater feel of the type of work that this advisor will do than people who have actually worked with the advisor. Be sure to call the referrals and take good notes.

What is your area of expertise?

There are many advisors who may be very good at selecting investments, but maybe you are just looking for someone who can help you get out of debt, improve your credit, and budget responsibly. Make sure that you list and prioritize your financial goals and needs – college planning, cash flow management, insurance planning, retirement, investment, etc.

How long have you been practicing in this area?

An advisor that has set up shop for five years or more will have established either a good or bad reputation by now.

What sort of clients do you serve?

It is good to have a planner that deals with clients with similar needs and income levels as you.

What is your investment philosophy?

Every advisor has an investment philosophy whether it is aggressive, conservative, or mixed. If you feel that he is a wild cowboy trader and you are looking for someone who is very conservative you probably shouldn't pursue it any further.

Do you practice community outreach?

If you want to know if an advisor is in it for the money or for the cause of empowering people with the important principles of fiscal responsibility, get an overview of their community outreach. If they are willing to teach people this information for free, the more likely they are to be in it because they have the heart to empower people than they are in it just to make a quick dollar.

There are many companies that are run like a multi-level marketing company. Your advisor should not also be in the business of trying to make you an advisor in their "down line" so they can make a percentage of your sales. Imagine if a lawyer defended you in court then after the case was concluded, they give you a six week course to obtain your JD (law degree) so you can practice under him and he gets a percentage of all of your cases heard. This sounds ridiculous - because it is. Lawyers, doctors, accountants, and financial planners all need to have a proper education and training to be considered qualified.

Other Important Members of Your Advisory Team

The following are also important members of an advisory team that you should consider:

1. **Bookkeeper** – This person handles all of your monthly bank statements and reconciles your account. If you don't have a business than you can do this for yourself. However, if you do have a business and it is in your budget to pay someone to do this for you it is definitely worth relieving the stress. The stress of keeping track of your receipts and summarizing your accounts is one something I am sure that you can live without if you can afford it.

2. **Accountant** – Whether you own a business or not you need a good accountant. Many people think that they can go to the "cookie cutter" accounting agencies, which can be okay for those with simple tax returns; but I always prefer to go to someone who can give you a little more individual attention. If you have a business you need to find someone who can advise you on all the deductions that you are allowed under law. Below are a few tips on how to find a good accountant.

a. Get Referrals

b. Find a CPA (A good resource for this is to search online at the American Institute of Certified Public Accountants at www.aicpa.org.)

c. Conduct Interviews – Some questions to ask are:

- How long have you been a CPA and how long have you practiced?

- What school did you graduate from?

- Have you ever worked with the IRS?

- Can you assist me in an audit?

- What software do you use to do my taxes and do you backup your work in case your computer crashes?

- How much do you charge?

- Are you the primary person who will be doing my taxes? If so will I be able to get in contact with you during the busy season… do you have some help?

3. **Personal Banker** – If you don't have a business this can be done yourself; however, if you do have a business you should use this service to discuss lines of credit and various tools that you can use for your business. They can help you set up your account, establish a business line of credit, and many will want to assist you in opening an investment account (I would leave the investing to your financial planner as they will more likely give you individualized attention).

4. **Attorney** – Everybody needs a good attorney in their speed dial just in case something happens.

   a. **Estate Planner** – An easy way to find an estate planner is through referrals. If you don't have anybody who can give you a good referral I like using the National Association of Estate Planners and Councils. Your estate planner should be an Accredited Estate Planner (AEP) and/or an Estate Planning Law Specialist (EPLS) if your estate is more complex in size (over $2 million in assets) and might need more than a simple will.

   b. **Corporate** – If you have a business you should have a good corporate attorney. Be sure to get a few referrals, have a meeting with them, and ask about their educational background.

   c. **Criminal** – You never know what sort of trouble lies ahead. I have had friends who were falsely accused of things give me a call because they know that I know good attorneys willing to help.

5. **Real Estate Agent** – A good real estate agent can be very valuable to have when you decide to purchase a home. Below is a check list of those things that you should look for in a good agent:

   a. **A good agent will:**
   - Help you focus and analyze your market.
   - Set up appointments for you to view prospective homes.

- Accompany you on your visit.
- Coordinate certain aspects of the transaction.

b. **A good agent is:**

- Working full-time as an agent.
- Experienced in the types of services you require.
- Full of integrity.
- A local resident.
- Able to communicate effectively.
- Always accessible and reliable.
- Sensitive to your needs.
- Able to produce a multiple listing service of the area.

c. **You must always:**

- Interview your agent.
- Ask for references.

APPENDIX D

5 MINUTE CHECKLIST

Please take a few minutes to complete this checklist. Any "no" or "not sure" answers can point to potential problems you may wish to inquire about via personal consultation.

Wealth Management Principles

Can you tell/show me your monthly expenses? ❑ Y ❑ N ❑ Not sure

Are you on track to fund your retirement? ❑ Y ❑ N ❑ Not sure

Are your investments well diversified? ❑ Y ❑ N ❑ Not sure

Have you written down all your financial goals? ❑ Y ❑ N ❑ Not sure

Is your tax return each year too high? ❑ Y ❑ N ❑ Not sure

Do you have too much insurance according to needs? ❏ Y ❏ N ❏ Not sure

Is your estate plan (will, trust, living will, etc.) up to date? ❏ Y ❏ N ❏ Not sure

Your Team of Advisors

Do you talk to all your advisors at least monthly? ❏ Y ❏ N ❏ Not sure

Are your advisors independent of one another? ❏ Y ❏ N ❏ Not sure

Do you know the fee structure of all your advisors? ❏ Y ❏ N ❏ Not sure

Did you do a background check of all your advisors? ❏ Y ❏ N ❏ Not sure

Managing Your Family and Friends

Have you communicated your $ goals with your family? ❏ Y ❏ N ❏ Not sure

Have you met with your family to tell them your $ plans? ❏ Y ❏ N ❏ Not sure

Transitioning: Life After Sports

Have you expanded your network of friends/colleagues with people who can empower you? ❑ Y ❑ N ❑ Not sure

Do you have a 3rd party that can help you analyze all investment opportunities objectively? ❑ Y ❑ N ❑ Not sure

Have you continued to pursue educational resources? ❑ Y ❑ N ❑ Not sure

Making an Impact

Do you have a cause you would like to champion? ❑ Y ❑ N ❑ Not sure

Can you support your cause w/o forming a foundation? ❑ Y ❑ N ❑ Not sure

Do you have a written plan to make an impact? ❑ Y ❑ N ❑ Not sure

Calculations: Have Your Financial Advisor Assist You With Calculations If Assistance Is Needed

What is your estimated net worth? _____

What are your estimated annual living expenses? _____

Financial Security = Having a net worth at least 20x your annual living expenses.

Is your net worth at least 20x your living expenses?   ❑ Y   ❑ N   ❑ Not sure

What is 10% of your gross income? _____

Can you support yourself on 10% of gross income and save the remainder?   ❑ Y   ❑ N   ❑ Not sure

Estimated Financial Savings Goal:

Your Annual Living Expenses/ 5% _____

Made in the USA
Middletown, DE
23 February 2022

61716175R00046